MW00929561

LETTERS FROM RED CLAY COUNTRY

Selected columns

By Mark Wallace Maguire

Published by Speckled Leaf Press

Published in the United States

ISBN-13: 978-1516987818

Author's Note:

In what order does one publish a book of columns?
Should it be chronologically? By theme? By intent?
I chose to publish them by season, which, at the outset,
might sound a bit odd, but the more I read through them,
they made sense in that order. That said, you will notice that
ages and dates are not always sequential, but I believe the book
flows better as a whole. I begin in fall, which, while not the
beginning of the calendar year, marks, in many ways,
the start of a new year with school cranking back up,
the end of vacations, social activities resuming and, of course,
that Southern staple known as football.
Except for slight edits, these columns appear as they were published.
A thanks goes out to the readers who encouraged me
through the years with their letters, emails, phone calls
and conversations in the aisles of the grocery stores,
churches and at sporting events. I always appreciate
your input and it keeps the fire burning.
Also, a special thanks to my uncle, Mike Maguire, for
his encouragement in this venture.

These columns originally appeared in Cobb Life magazine,
Cherokee Life magazine and Neighbor Newspapers, Inc.
of Times Journal, Inc.
Special thanks to Times Journal, Inc.
for allowing these columns to be reprinted.

First...
and the Five-Year-Old

2011 marked the first time when my oldest son Patrick, now 6, actually watched, and I mean really watched part of a football game with me.

Previously, he had feigned interest, primarily I believe to indulge in some tailgating food and to use the game as an excuse to run through the house and yard yelling, "Touchdown!" and "Go Dawgs!" at the top of his lungs.

But the few moments he did watch some of the games, his perspective proved enlightening.

Whenever a player ran or caught a pass, he yelled, "Touchdown!" I had to inform him that a first down wasn't necessarily a touchdown, but I did encourage him to keep cheering.

Like most boys, he mimicked my enthusiasm and even if the play was a simple two yards and a cloud of dust, he would jump up and down and yell, "Go! Go! Go!"

Being a passionate fellow, he brought a very intense level of emotion to each game.

In particular, I recall the UGA-Vanderbilt game. At one point in the first quarter, he had an angry look on his face and his eyes were welled with tears. He was pointing at the television yelling, "Stop! Stop!"

When I asked him what was wrong, he said the TV shouldn't be showing the Vanderbilt players at all, because they were "the bad guys."

I let him know that though we wanted to win the game, they still had to show players on both teams. It was also during that game that he noticed flags.

"What's that, Daddy? Why are they throwing flags? Why are the flags yellow and not red, white and blue?"

I explained to him about penalties, and, unfortunately used the phrase "illegal formation."

"Illegal?" he asked, his voice bordering on tears. "Are they taking the Georgia players to jail?"

I stifled my laughter, not wanting him to feel that I was mocking him and tried to explain what I meant by "illegal." I worked my brain to find all the synonyms I could – unfair, out-of-place, against the rules and, yes, let him know no one was going to jail over a football play.

Throughout the season, his questions only increased to levels light years beyond the average fan.

"Hey Daddy, what if Georgia played the Atlanta Falcons? Who would we want to win?"

Georgia.

"Hey Daddy, what if Auburn played LSU? Who would you want to win?"

That depends on how much grass Les Miles is eating this year.

And my favorite: "Hey Daddy, if Georgia played the Jedis who would win?"

That answer at least was simple. With lightsabers and The Force, a Jedi football team would be unstoppable.

Toward the end of the season a strange thing happened. My son – a descendant of many UGA alum and football players – informed me his favorite team now was LSU.

"Why is that?" I asked.

"I don't know. I like LSU."

I chalked it up to his kindergarten teacher being an LSU fan and Patrick developing a slight crush on her.

I told him that was fine. He could like LSU, just not to root against Georgia, since, after all, he lives in my house. The LSU fascination thankfully only lasted about three weeks. Over the summer, he deepened his passion for UGA and I also worked with him on his expression for other teams. What do I mean?

Simple.

When he said he hated LSU, I would tell him not to use the word "hate," but perhaps instead say, "I don't care for it."

Apparently, he thought that phrase was too polite for football.

"Daddy, what if I say they smell?" That works. Since then, he has refined his descriptions for feelings of teams.

"Pee-uuu. LSU smells."

"Daddy, why does Alabama smell so awful?" And the gentler, in deference to friends and relatives from the Orange Nation.

"Tennessee has some great people, but a smelly football team."

These aren't the most eloquent phrases, but they are, unfortunately, a lot more diplomatic than what you will hear from most SEC fans these days.

And, to be honest, they are a lot nicer than what I will express when I lock myself in my man room during a football game and preach the old mantra, "Do as I say, not as I do."

Patrick still hasn't watched a whole quarter of football with me and that's fine. There will be plenty of time for him to take a game too seriously as he grows up.

In the meantime, I will settle for questions about "Star Wars" characters playing in Sanford Stadium and the varying degrees of odors that emanate from other football teams.

20 Things I'd Like to Say Before I Die

S o Forbes put out a list of "40 things to say before you die."
It was a twist on the traditional bucket list idea, but with some interesting and, occasionally obvious, insights into how our words define our existence. Suggestions and tips had a bit of a "Tuesdays with Morrie" type feel — and I mean that with no disrespect — and were put forth so we could all define our lives in better terms.

Suggestions were along the line of, "Today was good" or "I can do better" or "This is wrong." Each phrase had a self-helpish explanatory sentence with it, demonstrating how saying these words will benefit your life. Of course, I was inspired and developed a much less intellectual, yet just as important list of my own.

While these are not exactly things you should say before you die, I define my list as "20 things I'd like to say before I die." And while this is my list, I do believe some of these sentiments to be universal. Here you go:

1. This is a hard choice, son, but life is about choices. Oxford has the better reputation, but Harvard is closer to home. Either way you're getting a full scholarship, so I support you in whatever decision you make.

2. Strange, even after winning three national titles in five years, watching UGA play football never gets old.

3. I cannot believe all the money that was donated this year to help the poor, the needy and the disabled!

4. What shall we drive tonight, dear? The Aston Martin or the Stingray? The Rolls is in the shop again.

5. What a great sermon! That makes two weeks in a row!

6. So, this is how earth looks from space.

7. A model? Me? I never really thought about it, but, go ahead, I'm listening.

8. I never thought I would get to play a $25,000 guitar.

9. There is absolutely nothing left to be fixed or to be cleaned in the house.

10. Film option rights? For my life story? How many millions did you say?

11. I am truly flattered, Ms. Klum, but I am a married man.

12. I don't need a nap.

13. Did you see this latest study? It says that scientists have proven that biscuits and gravy are good for your heart, brain, joints, lower cholesterol and help stave off all forms of cancer.

14. Well, I can't speak for everyone, but I am thrilled the college football season now runs from August to February.

15. There's more beer left? I thought we were out.

16. It took a long time, but I, too, am happy that our country is finally energy independent.

17. We didn't expect our son to make the jump to the NBA after one year of college either, but he can always go back and finish his degree. In the meantime, I'm enjoying early retirement.

18. It is great to see the turn that society has made and evolved into a much more civil and respectful place.

19. I sure do love this new ban on cell phones in restaurants. What a great idea.

20. I have seen more miracles happen in this life than I ever anticipated, expected or dreamed.

EAT FIRST,
ask questions later

I t was a hole in the wall Jamaican restaurant in Smyrna on South Cobb Drive.
It closed roughly a decade ago, when police discovered they were selling marijuana out of the kitchen.

But when I went in 1998, it was gaining the reputation as an authentic Jamaican style food stop in the then rather bland Smyrna restaurant scene.

I had developed a liking for Jamaican food through the years. One of my roommates in college hailed from Kingston, the capitol of that island nation, and his mother would mail us huge jars of homemade jerk sauce we slathered on chicken breasts. I would also occasionally eat at Atlanta's Bridgetown Grill where their Anglicized Jamaican food was still pretty tasty.

So when my friend Jonathan Meely and I set out to that restaurant one evening 13 years ago I had high hopes for scoring a good dinner. Walking into the restaurant I immediately felt it was the real deal. Though sparsely crowded, the air was thick with Caribbean accents punctuating the air. A soccer game played on an old television set sitting on a table and the walls were covered with faded Air Jamaica posters. I was also the only white guy in the place, (Jonathan is African-American and we played in a musical duo called Rice and Gravy,) and I felt I must have discovered a real gem.

We both ordered a combo plate that came with our choice of soup. The most intriguing soup on the menu was called Mannish Water. According to the description, it consisted of meat, yam, potato, bananas and dumplings. It sounded new and interesting and the name itself had me feeling like a muscular member of Bob Marley's band so we both ordered it.

It was an interesting soup, rather bland with small bits of vegetables and a watery broth. But there was one exception: A rubbery, honey-combed textured piece of something in the bowl. Not wanting to appear ignorant and wanting to keep up my self-professed coolness (ego is tough pill to swallow) I did not ask what it was and forced myself to swallow it.

The rest of the meal was forgetful. I think I had a half a jerk chicken with the obligatory rice and peas. I can't recall what Jonathan ordered. Later when we got back to his place to play some music, I had to ask him what the rubbery, honey-combed ingredient was.

Our conversation went something like this.

"Hey, by the way, what exactly was that strange, rubbery thing in the Mannish Water?"

"Heck, I don't know. You're the cultured white boy, I thought you knew these things."

"I have no idea what that was. Those are your people, I thought you knew what we were eating."

"Me? I have no idea. I just know whatever it was, it was nasty."

We both gave an uneasy laugh, then prompted by our curiosity, Jonathan made the phone call. I could only hear his end of the conversation, but it went something like this.

"Yeah, we were up there eating earlier and had the Mannish Water.....yeah, that was us. Hey what was the honeycombed, rubbery, meaty stuff in there?"

I heard a muffled reply.

"What, did you say goat?" Jonathan asked.

Goat, I thought?

Another muffled reply.

"The gut of the goat? We ate the gut of a goat? Do you mean goat chitlins?" Jonathan looked at me, his eyes wide, a look of merriment on his face.

"What do you mean we weren't supposed to eat it? It's just for seasoning!"

He hung up.

Stared at me.

"Maguire, we just ate goat chitlins."

I uttered a word I won't reprint and we both dashed into his kitchen where we gulped down a few shots of liquor in hopes that it would kill any strange goat-like bacteria lurking in our system. I felt okay the rest of the night, though that could be chalked up to the amounts of alcohol I consumed to kill any goat germs.

Since then, I look back fondly on eating the "gut of a goat." But that experience combined with a rough time at an Ethiopian restaurant in Doraville weaned me off of the authentic food kick. Instead, I decided to stick with the straight and narrow and fill my tummy with food from Celtic and European roots.

That was until now.

Recently, I was fortunate enough to be on location for a few of the international restaurant features in the magazine and am happy to report that, after sampling the fine cuisine offered, I am back on the global food venture. The cuisine served at these restaurants was outstanding across the board, rich with tastes and flavor and altogether a wonderful retreat from everyday food. All the chefs were beyond friendly and there were no strange ingredients lurking in the soups.

So, I've opened my mind back up.

A little.

But, one thing I've learned.

No more eat first and ask questions later.

Remembering Larry Munson

I was privileged enough to be at the UGA-Kentucky game this past weekend when the Dawgs clinched the SEC East and punched a ticket to the conference title game.

It was a beautiful day, perhaps the best football weather I've ever experienced in over 30 years of watching the Dawgs play in that paragon of a beautiful stadium. The sun broke through a chilly overcast morning and gave us a dazzling sunny afternoon where by the end of the first half, many of the fans around me were shedding coats and sweaters to bask in the September-like warmth.

Halfway through the first quarter, I noticed starting tailback Isaiah Crowell wasn't running anymore and back-up Carlton Thomas, who the week prior had notched a career-high game, was not on the field either.

Instead, the small, but speedy Brandon Harton had lined up in the running back spot.

My friends and I discussed it briefly.

"Had anybody seen anything?"

"Could you see what is going on down at the sidelines?"

"I didn't see an injury, did you?"

That was when I turned around in my seat and tried to spy anyone with a pair of earphones and a radio listening to the game. My search turned up nothing. I turned back in my seat and announced to my seat mates.

"Funny. Growing up, half of the men here would have earphones on so they could listen to Munson call the game and I could ask one of them to get the scoop. Now, I guess I will have to wait until someone dials up something on their phone."

That observation sums up the devotion UGA fans had to longtime Dawg broadcaster Larry Munson. Going to UGA games growing up, it was par for the course to see hundreds of fans show up at Sanford Stadium with not only their red and black donned, but with radios and headphones as well so they could listen to the voice of the great broadcaster

And though Munson left the booth a few years ago, that is why his death earlier this week still had folks across the state and the nation sharing tributes and memories of the man and his amazing talent.

I wanted to capture a bit of that in this column, but it isn't easy.

It is simply tough to communicate words about a communicator of words. It just doesn't feel right in a way, but I would be missing an opportunity to salute a great man if I did not.

Munson's use of the English language, his passion and his descriptions are unparalleled. And he did it all without a script or editing. His talent revealed itself in real time. I do rank him as a talented and unique wordsmith up there with the best.

And I do not say that lightly. In my man room, I have photographs of many great writers hanging on the walls. Among the visages of Ernest Hemingway, T.S. Eliot and C.S. Lewis is, you guessed it, Larry Munson.

Like thousands of other fans, I turned down the volume on the TV and turned up the radio to listen to him call a game. (And, yes, even when he was ten seconds ahead of the play on TV, I would sacrifice watching a play develop to hear his voice.) But it was not just the game that he called, it was his apt descriptions of other things. The man described weather as well as anyone I have ever heard. I still remember phrases like, "dark clouds gathering over the west side of the stadium, the threat of rain picking up" or "gorgeous, just gorgeous day, but very windy. I ruined a cigar just standing in the end zone watching warm-ups."

Munson called UGA basketball for years and even had an outdoors show. I embarrassingly cannot remember him calling a basketball game, but would love to hear an outtake of one or one of his fishing shows.

One final Munson moment I'd like to share is about a good friend of mine who grew up an adamant Georgia Tech fan. We were in my car on the way back from an event in 2001 when he indulged me by listening along to the UGA-Tennessee game when Munson made his famous "hobnail boot" call. The call did it for him and after that moment, he became a UGA fan. He has watched dozens of Georgia games with me and, yes, was one of the friends I had sitting with me at last week's Kentucky game.

I can't really say much more than that, except thanks Larry.

THANKSGIVING
starts with a bang

My family usually celebrates Thanksgiving at my grandmother's home in Thomaston, a small, Norman Rockwell-esque town located in the serene pasture and hill country between Macon and Columbus.

At 84, my grandmother not only cooks several dishes, but still has the unique talent of assigning holiday tasks. As far back as I can remember, I have been charged with a variety of jobs including chopping celery, stirring gravy, taking out the trash, setting out tables, setting the table and, my new personal favorite, staying out of sight until the meal is ready.

Thanksgiving is not one of my favorite holidays. Not quite up there with, say, Christmas or St. Patrick's Day. But, it is one of those increasingly rare days when the family can just stop and spend time together.

Despite the change time brings to our lives, there are always certain traditions to fall back on as predictable as my grandmother having the Macy's parade turned on the TV when we walk through her front door. With two preachers in the Maguire family, you are guaranteed to hear a solid prayer before dinner and if my Aunt Lisa isn't filling in as a nurse at the hospital you are guaranteed to drink the best iced tea in the State of Georgia. In fact—as blasphemous as this sounds for a Southerner—it's so good that it's about the only iced tea I drink all year.

Sometime after the eating and the fellowship have ended, another tradition takes place—a football game among the cousins. With only two females born into the Maguire line in the past 80-plus years, the testosterone and trash-talking are easy to come by. Harder to come by is a football, but somehow a ball is always found and soon grown men are hurtling it through the crisp November air, trying to summon the strength and stamina of their youth.

I will probably throw a few respectable passes and make a few decent catches. Even more probable is the fact that I will stumble, run out of breath and, after a couple of games, forgo further embarrassment to engage in a sport at which I really excel—pie eating.

As the afternoon deepens into evening and the family thins out, we'll load the kids in the car and drive those haunting middle Georgia highways north toward I-75. As we pass pecan groves lit by lonely lights and old churches whose steeples pierce the chilly night, the afternoon's soreness will set in and I will inevitably confess to my wife, "I really shouldn't have done that… again."

With apologies to T.S. Eliot, this is how Thanksgiving usually ends, not with a bang, but with a whimper.

AMBUSH CAROLING
a favorite Christmas memory

The buses lined up one by one in front of the
church fellowship hall, expelling thick diesel fumes into
the winter night. Dozens of volunteer carolers boarded
the buses, their cheerful faces illuminated by the yellow
hue of streetlights.

It was Charlotte, NC, 1985, the week before Christ-
mas. My father was pastor at Pritchard Memorial Baptist
Church, a large downtown church, hugged by the bank-
ing district on one side and public housing on the other.
I was 12 years-old. And this is one of my favorite
Christmas memories.

Every year, the last Saturday evening before Christmas
my father would partner with the city of Charlotte to
secure four or five city buses for the church's use. Church
members (of which as a preacher's son I was always part
of) would show up at the fellowship hall shortly after dinner and get fueled on coffee, hot chocolate and donuts.
Then, after a brief prayer, we would separate into groups
and clamber onto the buses to be shuttled off into the
bitter cold.

The buses were bound for the homes of shut-ins, the
sick and the elderly who couldn't get out to celebrate or
indulge in the merriment of the season. A bus would pull
up in front of a house or nursing home and the would-
be carolers would file off. Then, without announcing our
presence, we would launch into a hearty rendition of
several Christmas carols.

The reaction was almost always the same, to a science.

Soon, a light would come on in the house or a curtain
in the den would be yanked back to see what the com-
motion was all about. Then a porch light would flicker

on and a figure would appear in the doorway. Sometimes, it was the shut-ins themselves who ambled to the door. Other times, a dutiful child or caretaker would crack the door. After taking in the shock of a crowd of unannounced carolers on their lawn, they would turn back inside to inform the other home's residence as to what the noise was.

We were always greeted with warm smiles, tears of joy, and an offer of cookies or an invite to come inside and get warm. But we had miles to go before we slept and, as our last number, left them with a rendition of "We Wish you a Merry Christmas" before getting back on the bus.

I can't recall the exact number of homes we visited each year, but it was enough to register strong thoughts in memory.

The tears of thankfulness and the happy shock on the faces has been etched in my mind and has always been for me the essence of what Christmas is really about: An ambush of joy, stealing into the dark, bearing hope and reminding the sick, the old and the grieving that they are not forgotten.

After a few hours of caroling, the buses would drive us back to the church, drop us off and stories would be exchanged over another round of hot chocolate and donuts.

I can still almost hear them now more than two decades later.

"Well, our group couldn't sing a lick, but we made up for it with exuberance."

"Mrs. Mitchell thought we were a bunch of drunks at first. She said she almost called the police until she recognized the preacher."

"I didn't think we would be able to leave Mrs. Parker's home. She sure was grateful."

On the Sunday morning before Christmas, the church sanctuary would be filled with the joyous strains of Handel and Bach. Two glittering Christmas trees towered in each corner and my father would deliver his sermon clad in a rare red sweater vest underneath his stern suit.

And while all the cheer, the lights and the music were otherworldly to the eyes of a 12 year-old, they paled in comparison to the magic of untrained voices delivered in a biting cold the night before.

The little things...
make such a big difference

From suit-clad business moguls to elementary school children, everyone turns their attention to common themes this time of year: Counting our blessings, telling those close to us that we love them and devoting time to reflect on the true meaning of the holiday season.

Though Thanksgiving generally takes the center stage for the 'What are you thankful for?' question, I also think about the question every Christmas. It provides me with an opportunity to reflect on the last year, remind myself of my blessings and, in general, re-adjust my perspective on life.

Some folks have grand items they are thankful for such as stock prices in their portfolio rising, a new luxury car or retirement on the horizon. Others of us drag out the tired, yet true phrases like family and health. And then there are those we know who have truly experienced something miraculous and are thankful for things like the unforeseen healing from disease, a new job or a prayer being answered.

These are all well, well-intentioned and good. But this year, I am scaling back in my focus. I am taking my eyes off the big picture and looking at the smaller things.

Here are ten things I am thankful for:

1. Coffee: This beautiful black elixir does not only make me a better person on a daily basis, but has also given me the power, strength and alertness to keep full-time employment.

2. Air-conditioning: It may have damaged the front porch culture of America, but in July after cutting the grass, there are few luxuries in life as much appreciated.

3. Ice: As in ice cubes for cold drinks on hot days. Enjoyed with air-conditioning.

4. Fingers, hands, arms, knees and toes: I am the prince of broken bones, having suffered over a dozen. The last time I broke my arm in 2011, I truly realized how much I not only relied on it, but loved it and needed it. It allows me to type, to do my job, to play guitar and to toss the ball with my sons. Thank you God for healing me.

5. A patio: Five years later and I still miss the back porch of our old home. But, I am grateful for a patio. A place to sit and repose and relax on the weekends, watching the cobalt blue edge into blackness until the stars make their entrance. There are few things as simple and sublime.

6. Homegrown vegetables: I have a special place in my heart, or rather palate, for fresh vegetables pulled from a local garden. This year reassured my love as the damp summer destroyed all of my tomatoes, cucumbers and peas. I really only had two good tomatoes all summer, brought to me from my friend Adam in Nashville. I praised him ceaselessly for it. I love a good vegetable from the rich Southern soil.

7. A car: I did not get my first car until I was 21. It is a long story, but it did make me appreciate the automobile that much more. I love riding my bike, but having the luxury of independent travel on four wheels is indeed a blessing.

8. Shoes: In poetry and romance movies, there is nothing as refreshing and wonderful as walking barefoot. And though the soles of one's feet may feel enchanted in a cool patch of zoysia, the grass also hides other things, namely rocks, sticks, thorns and more rocks.

9. A backyard: Many folks are not afforded this luxury. But the simple existence of a yard filled with birds and surrounded by a thicket of trees provides me with a sanctuary and a place for my boys to raise all types of Cain with pure abandonment.

10. Clean, running water: Think this is too easy of a choice? Okay, just read up on how our species kept clean and healthy for our first thousand of years on the planet. Then, do a little research into how many countries still lack this taken-for-granted resource.

Before the holidays are over, I encourage you to take a moment, dig a little deeper this year, discard the clichés, and count your blessings, great and small.

Re-discovering the Joy of Weather

A wind soared high above us, knocking a trio of pine trees together, their hollow banging sounding like a strange woodland incantation. Around us, pale winter sun left dappled patches of opaque light on the forest floor, lending a translucent light to the pine straw, the dead, matted patches of grass, the half-frozen mud.

It was a frigid afternoon and my son Patrick, then 5, and I were on a hike. Before we left the confines of our heater-fed home, the Weather Channel reported the wind chill factor at 11 degrees, a temperature that had most of our community huddled indoors. For me, the temperature meant one thing - ideal conditions for a hike.

Clear.

Crisp.

Pure.

It took some convincing for my wife to let Patrick accompany me. But after a brief discussion that human beings had been living in conditions colder than this for many a millennia, she acquiesced and bundled Patrick in so many layers he resembled the visage of Randy in "A Christmas Story." (It was a feat of strength itself to strap his bundled body into the car seat).

I have always relished a winter hike and wanted to share the experience with him. The nippy air, the stark trees, the lack of humidity and perhaps, even selfishly, the absence of other people.

I explained this to Patrick, noting how everyone else was "afraid of the cold, but we weren't."

He laughed.

"No, daddy," he replied. "The weather is not scary."

We walked a brisk mile and a half before he told me he was getting cold.

"Of course," I said. "Let's go home and get a nice cup of hot chocolate for you."

Less than 10 minutes later, he had his back to a roaring blaze in our fireplace, a steaming cup of hot chocolate cradled in his hand and a smile on his face. His mother kept pinching his fingers and marveling at how chilly they were and how red his cheeks were. Patrick said he was fine and happy.

I smiled.

He was not afraid of the cold.

Winter hikes are just one of many types of weather adventures I have introduced to my sons. I have always held a deep affinity for almost all things weather related – the fierce winds of March, the whispering breezes of September, the punishing rains of spring and the untamed thunderstorms of summer, to name a few.

In fact, I can't recall ever not liking the weather.

As an adult, I see that same affinity in other children, especially boys.

Boys like to jump in mud puddles. Boys like to play in the rain. Boys can ignore the heat if a good basketball game is being played or a sandbox war is at bay. Boys like to run outside on a windy day and try to fly a kite. In fact, my youngest son Andrew takes a Zen-like delight in being outside on windy days. He will sit on my lap, half-close his eyes and reach a level of contentment I envy. (I have seen few visions of God as pure as the simple smile on his face when the wind tousles his hair.)

Maybe I am just a washed-up transcendentalist bohemian naturalist, but I do hold fast that being outdoors in the weather is a pure, good medicine that is a stronger sedative than the television, the Internet or any self-help book.

Unfortunately, somewhere along the way, by the time we reach adulthood, most of us have lost that fascination with weather. Instead of wonder, we have complaints.

It is too cold.

It is too hot.

It is too windy.

It is too… everything.

We have become conditioned to our "steady as she goes" homes and want our weather tailor-made like the rest of our lives. We want our weather on demand and scold it when it does not cooperate with our plans — as if we have any right to admonish a natural phenomenon that has been part of the earth long before our ancestors were born.

I know I am the exception to the rule. I know because I do not see many of you out on winter hikes. I know because I have seen you peer out from behind your shades with a slight shock written on your faces as I played in the rain with my children. But, as we are on the cusp of entering a new season, I do encourage you to take a step back and re-examine weather. No longer see it as a nuisance, but an opportunity.

It is more than green and red blurbs on a television screen. It is more than a gauge that determines which day to wash your car.

It is a living, untamed beautiful thing.

Get out. Have fun. Reach out. Maybe you'll rediscover something you haven't felt since you were a child. If nothing else, you will have justification for an extra cup of hot chocolate or a cold Popsicle at the end of the day.

How Did I Live Without You?

As a man grows older, he finds certain things are almost indispensable.

I can't function without a minimum of eight cups of coffee each morning.

I've got to eat red meat at least once a week.

And I've got to get in a good hike at least every season to refresh my senses.

But, in the last year, a new item has been added to my list.

He is a long lost friend, whom I had almost forgotten. He made his way through my door near Christmas last year. And, while at the time, I was appreciative of him; it is only in the last few months that I've realized just how critical he is to my life.

We go almost everywhere together.

He only leaves my side when I sleep.

He is tough, strong and has never failed me or let me down.

He is my pocketknife.

Yes, I use my pocketknife so often I can't fathom how I lived without it before.

When I was a young boy, I had several of them.

In a drawer somewhere I still have a multi-bladed worn Cub Scout knife whose blades are rusty with neglect. I also recall a single blade thick knife that had a handle crafted from bone or ivory. My father had several. Folks used to give them to him as gifts and I thought it was the coolest thing in the world and often wondered why he didn't use them more.

What exactly he would "use them for," I really don't know looking back on it. For me, I used them to whittle, to cut pieces of rope and to take camping. Mainly, as every young boy then knew, it was fun just to have one.

But, through the years I forgot about them.

If you took a pocketknife to high school you would be suspended and when I went off to college they weren't exactly at the top of my list of things to carry.

It is only during the past few years that I realized I could use one. And that was generally when I was trying to cut a piece of cord, loosen a screw or open a box – with generally a key or kitchen knife – that someone, usually an older gentleman, would come to my rescue. They would flip their knife open, use it and then tuck it back into their pocket.

And that is how I stumbled back into owning a pocketknife.

Last year, we were hosting Christmas dinner at our home. Like many family get-togethers it was only at the last minute that my wife realized we were missing something. Specifically, we needed another table (Her family numbers almost 30). So, like the dutiful husband I am (and relieved to leave the holiday chaos for a while) I ventured to Wal-Mart and bought an inexpensive card table that came neatly stuffed into a cardboard box.

I drove back home and brought it through the door, feeling mighty victorious like a hunter returning with food. All was well until I had to open the box. Then jabbing at it with a car key and trying to suppress a litany of curses in front of my sons and in-laws, I heard a calm voice.

"Here, Mark, use this."

My brother-in-law, Lindsay Hathcock, a true Southern gentleman, was holding a Swiss Army Knife in the palm of his hand. I took it, flipped open a gleaming blade and in about a minute had the extra table set up in the den. I told Lindsay thanks and mentioned I had actually been thinking about getting a pocketknife sometime and lamented how it was becoming a lost tradition.

"When I was young, we used to trade them," he said.

I had not heard of that tradition, I told him, but thought it was a great idea.

"Maybe something to put in a column one day," I said.

Then he did the unexpected and gave me his pocketknife, the fine Swiss burgundy with the umpteen blades and solid design. I told him I couldn't take it, but it was hard to argue with him too much. After thanking Lindsay profusely, I put it in my pocket. It generally stayed in my pocket, until a week later when I slipped it on my key ring where it now stays close by most of the day.

I like having a pocketknife again. I think it is a great tradition for men to carry one.

Just don't bet on me trading it anytime soon.

Snow Resurrects Memories of
'The Western Flyer'

I spent a few years of my childhood growing up in the small city of Forest City, N.C., a quaint town nestled among the foothills of that fine state.

The main street of that town seemed to have everything a boy wanted.

There was Smith's Drugstore that had a long linoleum counter and polished steel stools ringed around it. You could pony up to the counter - the smell of burgers simmering and eggs cooking thick in the air - and order a Coke float or a handmade Cherry Coke. And I mean real Cherry Coke, with the cherry flavor drawn from its own syrup, the type that existed long before it became mass marketed in aluminum cans and plastic bottles.

Also on Main Street, sitting back from the road and framed by stately trees sat First Baptist Church of Forest City, where my father served as pastor.

It was a regal building, built with brick and stone that paid homage to the 19th century when it was constructed. I've been to more than 40 churches throughout America and parts of Europe and the architecture of First Baptist Church of Forest City is still close to the pinnacle of brilliance.

Main Street also featured the local newspaper, a handful of clothing shops and The Western Auto Store. Long before Wal-Marts dotted the landscape, small chain stores like Western Auto were part of the fabric of small town America. Part auto parts store, part hardware store, part general store, Western Auto sold a variety of auto parts, various household goods, bicycles, appliances and the one item that always caught my attention – sleds.

The shop had several real sleds on display.

And I mean real sleds, not the plastic models you see today.

These had steel runners on the bottom that you had to rub candle wax on to ensure maximum speed. The sled also had thick, laminated pieces of wood on top, a leather strap to help you steer at the front and, above all, they had names neatly hand-painted on them in red paint. My favorite was the "Western Flyer," a name that conjured speed and a sense of Old West danger.

My parents bought my brother and me a "Western Flyer" one Christmas and it proved to be a worthy investment. Our backyard was a sledder's dream and a mower's nightmare. It went out about 20 or so feet from the backdoor and then plummeted a gorgeous dangerous angle of over 100 feet to the bottom of the yard.

We got snow almost every winter, it seemed in Forest City, sometimes up to three or four times. One winter, in particular, we got well over half a foot. Far from the quiet hushedness of snow that poets write about (myself guilty at times) the neighborhood was alive with the sounds of children laughing, sleds rocketing down the street and in our backyard, where my brother and I whooped in an exultation of accomplishment after, and only after, we had survived the heart-stopping lightning fast ride to the bottom of the hill.

Every morning for what seemed like days on end, we would rise, eat a hot breakfast of oatmeal and hot chocolate, bundle up, wax the blades of the sled and get ready for another day of sledding.

We moved from Forest City a year or so after that winter. The rest of my pre-college days were spent among three cities in the mild piedmont of the Carolinas. During those years, snow ceased to be a regular occurrence, but instead a rare visitor. We would get a dusting every two or three years if we were lucky, but usually just an inch or so of ice. It was just enough to get the TV anchors excited, boost the sale of bread and milk at local stores and tempt enough self-proclaimed macho men to drive in it, a fact they would relish over later.

During those years, the "Western Flyer" became a relic in our garage where dust piled upon its once stately frame and its red letters faded. I don't know what happened to the sled, I imagine it was eventually sold in a garage sale or given away.

I write all this, because the last few years, the frequency of snow has changed here. My wife and I figured our five-year-old son Patrick has seen more snow in his time on the planet than we saw in the ten years prior to his birth combined.

He, and the members of his generation, have been blessed. They saw a White Christmas. They got an amazing several days off of school for real snow, not ice or sleet. And, Patrick got to sled when the area got blanketed in early January. I even joined him for several trips down our neighborhood hills, reliving a snapshot of my own childhood.

There was just one thing missing.

You guessed it.

"The Western Flyer."

Though I haven't seen a "Western Flyer" in over two decades, I might be able to still find one online. And with the weather we've been having the last few years or so, there is a chance we might get another snow as late as April.

If not, I can always reminiscence about it with a Cherry Coke.

The Apple, the Tree and Letting it Be

The phone rang on a Tuesday evening.

I didn't answer it. I always try not to. Excluding telemarketers, no one calls me at home. And I mean no one. My wife gets most of the calls. If one of my relatives call, they say hello, but then quite quickly ask for her. Even my oldest son, Patrick, gets more calls than me. Seriously. He is only eight, yet averages about a dozen or so calls each year, most from a friend who likes to call and tell jokes.

So when the phone rang that evening, I did what I usually do.

Not a dadgum thing. Steady as she goes. Stay the course. Keep the couch from moving. Let it ring.

Then I heard the voice. My son's voice singing in a gruff accent about Legos, Star Wars and Minecraft and God-knows-what-else to someone on the other end of the line. He came running into the den and, with a generous smile, handed me the phone. Of course, I didn't want it, but took it. The line was dead. Thank goodness they had hung up by then. I was not in the mood to tangle with a sales pitch.

I imagine some parents would be mad or concerned about the lack of social graces or politeness with a child answering the phone that way.

I wasn't.

Why?

He learned it from me.

In an effort to deter telemarketers, I've been answering the phone non-sensically since before he was born. I generally affect an Irish accent and say something to the effect of 'We'll be right over with the ice, but caught our neck in a mangle at Ballyquickshannon and O'Neal's cow broke his leg,' but I also conjure heavy Southern accents and tell the caller, when they ask for Mrs. Maguire something along the lines of, "How do you know my wife, you son of a goat? Why are you calling her? Where do you want to meet? How big a boy are you? Come on, let's go. I've been wanting to meet you!"

I also enjoy playing radio host. The conversation goes something like this:

"Hello, may I speak to Mr. Maguire."

"Hey, and you are our 21st caller. We've got that rewards package coming right up for you right after this song by Little Johnny and the Small Dogs. Make sure to turn down your radio, because you are live and on the air. What's your name, caller?"

Usually, with all these approaches, I get what I want: Dead silence.

But, then again, I can't be blamed for this habit.

I learned it from my father.

While he has more sense than I do, he always answered the phone with his standards, "Maguire International Airlines," "Maguire's bait shop," or "Linda Maguire's answering service."

I never questioned him about it. I just grew up thinking that was how you were supposed to answer the phone, especially if you needed to get a laugh, give a laugh or get rid of a telemarketer.

Did he learn it from his father?

Well, I had to do some digging on that. I loved my granddaddy deeply, but did not recall him exactly as a comic. He was the epitome of the John Wayne tough guy: All-State Quarterback at Athens High, UGA football player, heavily decorated World War II veteran and a longtime educator whose reputation for discipline earned him the nickname, "Mean Dean Maguire" when he worked at Georgia Southern.

I recalled his fondness for laughing and a good joke growing up, but his bulky form, deep voice and overall intimidation often played a greater role in creating a memory of a stern and solid man, rather than a jovial one.

I talked to my dad about it and he told me that, yes, my granddaddy possessed a deep sense of humor, but it was much more low-key. He introduced himself with quite a bit of self-depreciation as "Squire Maguire" or some other nickname and told my father — a one-time minister — that if he fell asleep in church it wasn't his fault that the preacher was bad and, yes, also did answer the phone with the occasional off-kilter greeting.

Where does that leave me? Well, I guess to back where it started. 'Do as I say, not as I do' is a good mantra when trying to enlighten one's children on kindness, refinement and learning from your mistakes. But, when it comes to possessing a sense of humor — especially when it is not aimed at putting anyone down — well, that's not a bad thing. And what could I tell him anyway? Don't answer the phone acting silly? No. I don't plan to change.

Let's just hope that Patrick doesn't answer the phone that way when the principal or a teacher inevitably calls. Or for that matter, let's hope I don't answer it that way.

Then again, it might help explain a lot.

Celebrate
everything?

A few years ago, my mom hung a sign over her kitchen sink that proclaims "Celebrate Everything!"

It is a kitschy sign with tin cutouts of smiling pilgrims, tacky Christmas trees, American flags and laughing Jack O' Lanterns.

I never gave the sign much thought, until I realized that, while my parents know how to throw a memorable party, they really don't celebrate everything.

In my home, however, we do celebrate more than your average holidays.

And I'm starting to wonder if that is a good idea.

Before you cease reading any further, let me allay any fears to let you know I'm not talking about observing National Rhubarb Week or Paul and Linda McCartney's anniversary.

However, outside of the typical American holidays, we also commemorate St. Patrick's Day, St. Andrew's Day, Burns Night, the Feast day of C.S. Lewis (officially named recently by our Episcopal brethren), St. David's Day, Oktoberfest, St. Nicholas Day, Summer Solstice, Shrove Tuesday, the first night of Hanukkah, Chinese New Year and W.B. Yeats birthday.

Of course, in the fall, every Saturday is a celebration of sorts if the Dawgs are playing.

Toss in birthdays, anniversaries and half-birthdays and I ball-parked that we celebrate roughly 40 to 50 days a year.

That's great. One thing I learned from my dad is you can't rejoice enough when the occasion calls for it, because it doesn't happen enough in this life.

But herein lies the problem.

Most of the holidays revolve around food, music, traditions, drink and, of course, more food.

And most of the holidays I mentioned above tend to be Celtic or Northern European in nature.

The food for honoring those days – forgive me my fellow Celtic-Americans, but I must tell the truth – is simply awful.

I enjoy a corned beef and a bowl of hearty lamb stew a couple of times a year, but more than one Irish holiday a year and you are up the creek unless you want to consume nothing but potatoes, salmon and Guinness.

Plus, have you really ever tried to cook something special Scottish-related? Good Night! It is virtually impossible. We attempted to cook several recipes before I finally threw in the towel last winter and settled on sipping Scottish ale instead.

Then there is English food, for crying out loud. Yeah, I read enough food magazines to know there is a nouveau English cuisine movement in London at the moment, but for the most part, you're out of luck there as well.

Make a trip to Cap'n D's for fish and chips and count your blessings is all I can say.

Welsh food? Never heard of any. I always say the only good things to come out of Wales are Dylan Thomas and Catherine Zeta-Jones (and not in that order).

My point is I've got to find a new way to commemorate our holidays.

It got me thinking. Hot dogs, hamburgers and potato salad may not be the most complex fare on the planet, but this culinary trio may be getting serious consideration for our holiday food.

And, who is to say I still can't honor those days by enjoying a Scottish ale whilst thinking of Catherine Zeta-Jones and reciting W.B. Yeats?

Goodbye and Good Luck to the
WHITE-HAIRED WONDER

Though my family's roots are in Georgia, I spent roughly a decade of my life moving around the Tarheel state.

My dad, a die-hard UGA fan and Athens native, did what he could to follow UGA football. And, though we caught several games on national TV, it was still in the 1980s, pre-ESPN era and we had to glean most of our information from the Sunday morning newspaper.

Football being what it was - and with all apologies to North Carolinians - what it still is in that State, our family was baptized in the holy waters of that other great sport – college basketball.

My dad played basketball for his high school so he already had a great affinity for the sport. I had yet to discover my passion for it, but got my taste of its addictive nature from watching tons of ACC basketball games during the 1980s. ACC basketball then was what SEC football is now: Amazing, unbelievable, beyond talent-laden and simply the best.

Those were the glory years of ACC basketball. UNC was still playing in Carmichael Arena and names like Sam Perkins, Brad Daugherty, Jimmy Black, Warren Martin, James Worthy and, oh yeah, that Michael Jordan guy graced the courts with their presence.

Though I came to love the 'Heels, players on the other teams in that decade were also unforgettable. Spud Webb at N.C. State, Ralph Sampson at Virginia, Muggsy Bogues at Wake Forest, Mark Price and John Salley at Georgia Tech and a ton more.

And while the game for a kid like me was about watching the players, the incredible personalities and gravitas of the coaches themselves made an indelible mark.

With his strong Italian background and his unbridled emotions, Jim Valvano at North Carolina State was beyond charismatic.

North Carolina's Dean Smith came across as a wizened old wizard, usually composed, but always with a serious look with those narrow eyes and that unforgettable nose.

Duke's Mike Krzyzewski was just coming into the league, but his name alone was enough to garner attention.

And, then there was Georgia Tech's Bobby Cremins.

Though he was only in his 30s at the time, his hair was already just about all the way white. It was also, in accordance with the time, a bit shaggy and when he was upset it would swing back and forth producing the image of true mop top.

Cremins was great to watch. He wasn't as loose as Valvano (but who was?), but he was intense. He would bite his nails, bark out plays and sometimes just sit back with his chin in his hand studying the game. He also recruited, coached and produced some fantastic talent for Tech.

Mark Price was one of the best shooters I have ever seen, anywhere. John Salley was a beast in the paint. Dennis Scott, Brian Oliver and Kenny Anderson among many others always put on a show.

Cremins did well at Tech. His teams clinched three ACC titles and made deep runs into the NCAA tournament.

He also earned conference and national coach of the year honors. In 1990, the team made the Final Four. Along the way, Alexander Memorial Stadium earned the moniker "The Thrillerdome." Tech later named the court in his honor.

I was sad to see when Cremins left Tech in 2000 and retire - the first time - from coaching. I never have been a Tech fan, but I love good basketball. Good basketball is what Cremins produced.

I kept up peripherally with his career after that, watching his commentary on TV and catching the occasional interview with him on sports talk radio. I have to admit I was not surprised at all when he returned to coaching in 2006 at the College of Charleston. I was even less surprised with the success he had there, notching up around 20 victories a year. I am not a know-it-all, but those memories of his teams in the 1980s are burnt into my memory and good coaching is good coaching whether it is in downtown Atlanta or on the coast of South Carolina.

Earlier this year, Cremins alluded to retirement, citing exhaustion and telling folks he had run out of gas.

His official announcement Monday that he was leaving the sport was not shocking, but sad all the same.

But, I reckon at 64, with a basketball court named in your honor and a few hundred victories under your belt, it can be forgiven that you've run out of gas.

Good luck, Bobby, and thanks for all the memories.

Weather or Not,
...here the names come

A rose is a rose by any other name, the bard said, but at the same time, there is something to be said about the connotation of certain names, isn't there?

I really got to thinking on this after The Weather Channel began naming winter storms this year. After I got over my incredulity over naming winter storms (I mean, really, people?), I became impressed by their selection of monikers: Ion, Kronos, Hercules! Wow! Very strong and power-inducing names culled from mythology. I was impressed. Then, they introduced "Leon." Leon?

Really? I know it stems from "lion," but when I hear it, I don't exactly group it in the same arena as the other Greco-Roman storm names. I once knew a Leon. Easy going. Cool. Tough? Yes, but not in a "Clash of the Titans"-beastly-winter-storm way. In other words, not a guy I could see having a drink with Kronos.

Of course, they are doing better than the hurricane folks have been for the last several decades. They tend to use the blandest, most non-offensive names: Hazel, Camille, Katrina and such. It sounds like a gaggle of old spinsters sitting around playing bridge. And the male names aren't much better: Hugo and Floyd, for example. The only one that comes close to me is Andrew, but that is only because my youngest son is named Andrew and I have witnessed his mayhem and destruction up close and personal.

Then there were the winter storms and subsequent stranding we experienced this year that epitomized blandness. It was dubbed 'Snowpocalypse.' That was fine, I guess, but when the area was hit with a similar storm a few years ago, we called it 'Snowpocalypse' then, too. I was really disappointed in that. The Atlanta media couldn't come up with something more creative the second time around? If not a mythological name, perhaps something that sounds like a professional wrestler like Stone Cold Slap Down, The Great White Out, Snowstruck Strikeout or The White Dragon.

What's next in the weather naming world? High pollen counts called "Return of Old Yeller" or "Sinus Saffron Saturday?" Maybe they will start naming thunderstorms – that would be easy at least. Heat waves could be fun, but could border on offensive to get the right connotation with names like, "Sultry Susan," "Jezebel," "Swimsuit Cindy" or simply, "Kate Upton."

Oh well, in the end, a rose is a rose and I do enjoy language, but the more we name things, the less evocative power names have.

That said, it would do my ego good this summer to tell my out-of-state friends I was experiencing a case of the vapors from spending too much time outside with "Kate Upton."

SPRING

Not Home,
just the garden, please

I remember the books mainly. Two or three large coffee-table sized books would be strewn on the floor. My father and I sitting cross-legged as his measured voice read the directions aloud and I tried to follow the technical writing as best as I could.

They were the "Reader's Digest" Fix-it-Yourself books that were published in the late 70s and for a couple of years my dad tried to use them to fix minor problems around the house.

If there was a leaky pipe or broken faucet, he would grab one or two of the tomes, ask me to come with him and together with a handful of barely-used still shiny tools we would attempt to fix the problem.

The result was always the same - a miserable, frustrating failure that resulted in him confessing his screw-up to my mother followed by a phone call to the local plumber or handyman.

Why couldn't he fix things? Well, the man can read just fine. (He actually reads four languages and rips through a book or two a week).

The problem is, when it comes to anything mechanical, well, the talent just isn't there.

Never was.

Never will be.

Can't explain it.

Can't change it.

And, as the old cliché goes, the apple doesn't fall far from the tree. The only major difference between my dad and me is that I am slightly more proficient at fixing things and when I become frustrated, unlike him, I don't give up immediately and call a professional. Nope, instead I usually beat the stuffing out of whatever I am working on which inevitably results in an unhappy wife and a higher bill.

This is just one reason that in the past few years I have adopted the sage advice of UGA icon and garden pro Vince Dooley who once said something to the effect of his wife was in charge of domestic affairs –the house- and he was in charge of foreign affairs – the yard.

Yep, at home, my wife rules the house, including repairs, ideas for repairs, which she passes on to me to foul up, and calling for repairs. (And don't fret about my self-esteem; I'm way past the point of losing pride over this. I turned in my cape and ripped the "S" off my chest a long time ago.)

However, while she governs the inside, like Dooley, the yard is mine.

And there, I am happy. Gardening, planting and general landscaping has always provided me with a deep sense of gratification, of stress relief, of peace and bringing me closer to the Creator. Also, in the yard, I can plant almost anything and it grows. In the yard, I am talented. In the past few years,

I have planted more than 100 shrubs, bushes, plants and trees and, with the exception of one or two, they have all thrived. I simply do well with my fellow organic brothers and sisters. The only problem I have in the yard is the lawnmower and Weed eater, both of which have been replaced several times during the past few years after yours truly, usually more frustrated than usual from the heat, destroyed said machines.

But in the big picture, I still retain one advantage over my dad in my lack of mechanical aptitude. I am much more efficient. I save money and several hours by bypassing the fix-it books and diving straight into destruction.

'Happy Day'

In memory of Jay Whorton who passed away in March 2014

Dr. Jay. That's what most people called him. Dr. Jay.
There was also, 'The Doctor,' 'Jay-Bird' and, to his longtime friends, simply 'Jay.' And I called him Mr. Whorton a few times before he admonished me for my formality.

And then it was simply, 'Dr. Jay,' 'The Doctor' or 'Dr. Reverend Whorton' if we were in a mischievous mood, which was often when we went on one of our weekly lunches.

I knew Dr. Jay for over 15 years, but it was really only in the last ten that we got to know each other. What started out as a general business acquaintance evolved into a friendship. A friendship built on mutual respect, sharing truths with each other, empathy and on most days, having a similar sense of humor about this crazy life we all lead.

How does that happen? How does an 80-something-year-old outgoing, advertising guru become friends with someone half his age that has a tendency to be reserved with occasional forays into dourness? Because Dr. Jay was genuine. He was real. He was honest. He was interested in who you were. And he had that rare gift of being able to draw out a laugh in just about anyone. He always greeted you with an earnest smile, his booming voice and a handshake. For the ladies, he usually greeted them with "Happy Day" and for men, the words, "Hello, Brother."

And everyone was his brother.
His sister.
His friend.
His son.
His daughter.

The man, in many ways, had a tremendously large family. A family whom he loved and who loved him back.

Dr. Jay was not ashamed to tell people he grew up, "poor and on the mountain." He took pride in the fact he was a letterman at Jacksonville State University. He loved to tell how he married the most beautiful girl on campus - his longtime wife, Laura. He wanted you to know he worked for 40-plus years at the Marietta Daily Journal with his close friend and boss Mr. Brumby. And he loved to tell you stories upon stories. I have shelved dozens of his stories that include everything from his experiences at all-night wakes with the west Georgia gypsies to almost getting shot when, at the bequest of Mr. Brumby, he visited the penthouse of Howard Hughes.

There are many quotes and stories that reflect the type of person that Dr. Jay was. I have one in particular that defined him to me and what made him so special.

We were eating at the Marietta Diner a few years ago when a lady with a walker and an oxygen tank came lumbering by our table. Obviously struggling and in a bit of pain, Dr. Jay greeted her with a hearty, "You are looking good, lady!" She stopped and talked to us for a minute, relating her latest medical maladies. Dr. Jay listened, nodded and left her with a few words of encouragement. She smiled and thanked him. And it struck me. That is the good life. That is the way to live. That is the Christ-like life. Saying hello to one and all. Treating everyone with respect and love. Encouraging those around you. Making everyone feel loved, cared for and special. Wishing all a good morning, a happy day.

And, as many who knew Dr. Jay, the lady at the diner that day was not the only person he made a point of talking to. He made many people in the community have happy days. From the underdog to the top dog, he shook everyone's hand and made everyone feel unique.

He had a "special lady" - an adult with special needs - who worked cleaning tables at the Captain D's. He always made sure he saw her and always left her with a hefty tip. (And, no you are not wrong; you don't generally tip at Captain D's.)   He knew the two managers at a local Krystal's by name. Two African-American gentlemen he would always tell them he and his associate - this is when he would point to me - were going to buy them out, because "Krystal's has the best chili in town." No, he never did buy a Krystal's, but he left those two men always laughing and in good spirits.

And he harbored a deep affinity and focus on helping those in need.

The stories could go on and on.

Happy Day.

I'll miss my friend. I know I am not alone. We can talk about legacy. We can talk about impact. What does it mean? What is the purpose? What is our time on this earth good for? I don't know all the answers. But, in the end, if I can make one person smile everyday like Dr. Jay did, then that is a great way to be remembered.   Maybe, when you boil it all down to what really matters; it is the only way.

Thanks, Dr. Jay.

Happy Day.

Soccer and
a sign of the times

I have witnessed many signs of the apocalypse during the last decade.

I said I would never work for a newspaper, yet, have spent over 14 years in newspaper and magazine publishing. How did that happen?

Then I got married nine years ago -the forever-sworn-single rambling man made the jump.

Yep, definitely another sign of the end times approaching.

The wife and I bought a house. We were blessed with two sons. We bought a minivan.

Yep, all harbingers of the Four Horsemen on the horizon. All the things my wife had heard me say I would never do were coming true. Next, I was trading in reading time on biographies, theology and science fiction for colorful books about cows doing a barnyard dance and saying "Goodnight, Moon" and giving mice cookies.

The end was near.

I was sure.

This spring, another sign appeared.

I took my first coaching position. I would love to write that UNC basketball coach Roy Williams phoned me after hearing about my enlightenment in dissecting the triangle-and-two defense or UGA football coach Mark Richt invited me to join his staff because he wanted more trickeration in his offensive playbook.

Instead my first position was not as stellar in nature, but quite rewarding in and of itself.

I became the head coach of an Upward soccer team. The "head coach" moniker in itself did not freak me out so much. It was the word "soccer" that threw me for a loop. I enjoy watching the World Cup, but otherwise, soccer is a bit foreign to me. I was never coordinated enough with my feet or fast enough to decipher the intricacies of the game and play on any level, and I don't know or understand all the nuances and rules of the game. (Something in my nature likes sports where you can hit the other players so I stuck to basketball and football.)

But when my six-year-old son Patrick's soccer team needed a coach, well, a void needed to be filled.

A team needs a coach. Nobody else was stepping up. And it is darn near impossible to turn down five- and six-year olds.

So this fool stepped up to fill it.

I learned a few things.

There is a reason my father told me to never coach your own son. It is tough. To Patrick's credit, he always called me "Coach" on the field and his only faults were being too emotional and narrating his own plays. (Yes, one of his future jobs he told me, in addition to being a fireman and policeman, is to work for ESPN). My fault was being too tough on him. I actually had to let the referee know in one game that if I seemed super hard on one kid in particular, it was for a simple reason – he was my son. I didn't want to get tossed out of Upward Soccer for being a hard-nose, so I eased back and asked our assistant coach to work more with Patrick, instead of me.

I learned that, thankfully, in the 5 and 6-year-old level, you don't have to know all the rules. They just kind of herd around the field and you follow them and constantly tell them to space out, shoot at the right goal, not cry and pay attention to where the ball is more than the butterflies.

I also learned that when you ask things like, "Does anyone have any questions?" during halftime, you need to be prepared for anything. My favorite being, "Yes coach, I have a question. Do lions have babies?" Of course, the best part of coaching is just seeing kids celebrate and have fun.

I can't tell you I mastered the basics of soccer in one season, but I taught the kids the proper way to give a high-five and a belly bump. I couldn't tell you all the secrets of the game, but I gave a heck of a pre-game speech. I imagine this will be my one-and-done season as a soccer coach.

This dog is getting too old to learn new sports.

But, I also get an inkling that if Patrick plays basketball this fall and they need a spot filled, I will be there whistle and all, doing my best in a sport I do know.

I will also keep looking over my shoulder for the Four Horsemen. With the year 2012 already filled with fear and yours truly running madly on a soccer field, it might be sooner than you think.

Letting the cat out of the LUNCHBOX

My mother was busy ushering my brother and me out the door to her Plymouth Duster to tote us to school when I made the discovery. There in the black backseat of the car was our cat, a beautiful sweet calico, named Tinkerbell.

She lay on her side with what appeared to be four or five mice nestled up against her matted fur.

"Mom," I remember calling, "hurry, something is wrong with Tinkerbell!"

My 8-year-old mind had not quite reached its apex in biology and did not realize that the close-to-hairless tiny beasts that I thought were mice were actually kittens that were nursing.

Tinkerbell, our family cat, had given birth to a

litter.

In the back of my mom's car.

While our family had slept during the night.

And, as strange as it sounds, giving birth was actually one of the least traumatic events of Tinkerbell's life.

Tinkerbell was one tough mama.

My brother Jonathan and I were not cruel to her by any means, but like any young boys with pets we had to include her in all our adventures.

She followed us on hikes in the woods around our house, went sledding with us and we took her a warm saucer of milk every night.

But, the most memorable event was when we tried to put her into a lunchbox. She was quite cooperative, probably as curious as we were if she could fit in there. Our plan was to toss the lunchbox into the air—the lid not closed—and see, if by her amazing cat powers, she could still use her equilibrium to land on her feet.

Well, that never quite happened. Tinkerbell was too big to fit in the lunchbox. That was when my brother commenced to tossing the lunchbox as high as he could. It eventually landed on our neighbor's roof. That stunt earned him a mention in a local newspaper column. (This was not exactly the most glorious beginning for my brother's media attention-he has appeared on Atlanta television a couple of times as an expert in home construction-but that was his first claim to fame.)

But, back to Tinkerbell and her kittens.

We gave most of the kittens away, except an orange one.

This kitten became my brother's and he named her Clemson.

That would've been fine in some households, but was not exactly a hit with my dad. Over half of the Maguire family has graduated from the University of Georgia dating back 70 years. In other words, naming anything Clemson was bad.

Of course, to force a 5-year-old to rename a cat would not exactly be nice either, so my dad relented. And that was okay. My dad didn't like cats anyway and paid them little heed of mind.

We had Tinkerbell and Clemson as part of our family for a few years, but after we moved from a small town in the North Carolina foothills to the busy city of Charlotte they both succumbed to the same end—they were hit by cars.

We never did have any pets after that. I begged repeatedly for a dog, but my dad wouldn't have it. He didn't believe in chaining a dog and refused to buy one unless we had a fenced-in-backyard.

We never got a fenced-in-backyard or a dog. Now my oldest son, Patrick, has been asking about a pet.

When I asked him if he wanted a dog or a cat, he said neither.

He wants a deer.

I suppose when he and his brother, Andrew, are old enough I will get them a dog.

Little boys need dogs, I believe, and, as I am discovering, daddies always need more friends (I could especially use a good dog to keep me company in my man room on Friday and Saturday nights.)

My long term plan is to eventually move to the country and perhaps get a few pets.

I would like to watch a llama dot across the landscape just for kicks.

I could enjoy having a horse around, though I wouldn't enjoy doing the stable work.

My dream, though, is to get a falcon and become a falconer.

I want to send those noble birds out from my arm and have them retrieve all manner of rodents.

If I had falcons, I also wouldn't have to worry about them giving birth in the backseats of cars.

And that might delay me having to explain about the birds and the bees for a little bit.

Simple Pleasures We Enjoy on Memorial Day Due to Veterans

I will never forget discussing war with a politician years ago in a neighboring county when I was a cub reporter. We were talking about World War II and he remarked, "Those were great days, great days." I was so shocked to hear it described in that way, I followed up with a question as to where he served. He had not tasted the grit of the desert of North Africa, flown nightmarish missions over Germany or island-hopped in the Pacific. He was part of the clean-up crew that went in afterwards. In his own words, his war memories were peppered with girls in Italy, wine in France and games of Ping Pong. I do not disparage his service, especially since I myself have none to speak of, but the gallant mirth in which he spoke about the war irked me.

I do not tell this story to diminish any of our veterans' service. It just seems on a larger scale that "great days" is what Memorial Day has become. Simply nothing more than a chance to break out the grill, throw a party and release the white clothes from the closet. The truth is Memorial Day is so much more.

For me, it is about my two grandfathers. One who swore he would never get in a plane again after his B-17 crash-landed twice in England coming back from air raids over Germany. Another who saw action on the ground in the Korean War.

It is about Washington's rag-tag army that we have romanticized in words and paintings where we gloss over the fact that many of the soldiers were often sick, under-trained, unpaid and shoeless. It is about the veterans of our less popular wars (I use the term 'less' instead of 'un' because is any war ever popular?) like Vietnam and the Gulf Wars who return to a seemingly numb public unwilling or unable to hear their stories.

But I do know that we have lost a ton of respect in the country for our veterans. We make violence easy and clean in our video-game and cable-TV culture, yet seem to pay little heed to the ones doing the real work. The truth is, their work doesn't change. It is still real, often dirty and takes a toll.

I don't believe you can find true illumination in a Hollywood movie, but I do know that if you haven't seen, "Saving Private Ryan," or "Flags of our Fathers" Memorial Day is a prime time for these. If nothing else, take a moment when you fire up the grill or take a bite into a hot dog to remember that great sacrifices were paid to make simple pleasures as these possible.

What's on your
Summer Bucket List?

Since January, we'd been waiting for summer.
It arrived on Memorial Day weekend. And the rituals, along with a
dose of pandemonium, are under way.

The scent of charcoal smoke is on the breeze. Shorts and sandals
emerge after a long hibernation at the bottom of closets. You can hear
the voices of children playing outside through the last slivers of day-
light. Lightning bugs punctuate the darkness. Then come the camps.
Day camps, sports camps, art camps, vacation Bible schools. Maybe a
church event, perhaps a homecoming or revival. July the Fourth. Ice
cream. Fresh tomatoes, cucumbers, watermelon, corn. Cookouts. Pool
parties. Beach trips. Braves' baseball.

A doldrums of the weeks before school starts again when every mom
I know is past the point of losing patience.

And then, after the mad scurry, suddenly – it ends.

Over.

That seems to be the way it goes every summer, especially the older
one gets, doesn't it?

We make a rush of a time meant to be relaxing.

And, trust me, I don't say this as a cold critic or one who is completely
immune.

At the end of summer, I generally find myself bemoaning all the
things I wanted to do, but didn't. With that said, this year, I have written
a summer bucket list to make sure I do not find myself in that state of
mind again.

1. Make homemade ice cream: Growing up, this was a tradition in
my family. My parents loved to set our loud rock salt-laden maker on
the porch and my grandparents even had a hand-cranked one.

My wife and I half-heartedly carried the tradition on for a few years before fizzling out last summer. But this summer I am aiming for not one, but at least two bouts of homemade ice cream.

2. Wade in a stream: My family usually goes to Callaway Gardens at least once a summer and, though I don't swim, I will dip my feet in Robin Lake. But finding a good stream to wade your feet in is something I miss. I have a couple of fishing spots I've discovered here and there, but the key is to find the right amount of depth and current. When you do, there are few things as simply sublime.

3. The non-contact sports: Last year I played horseshoes for the first time at, ironically, an end-of-summer party. I tossed a few games – or is it matches? – and found it to my liking. Why? Well, I don't really care for croquet or golf. Secondly, you can play horseshoes with a drink in your hand and wear about anything you dadgum want to. (I prefer a Larry Bird T-shirt, seersucker shorts and a straw hat.) I might also give badminton another try. I played it when I was a child with my brother and cousins at my grandparents' home and I harbor fond memories of racing back and forth on the thick zoysia grass, trying to hit the shuttlecock while not getting blinded by the sun. Tennis is in the mix too. As long as it doesn't bode for broken bones, I am game.

4. Moonlight hike: When I was in my teens and early 20s, I frequently took midnight bike rides. It might sound foolhardy, but if you lived in the right place and knew which vacated roads to ride, it was a rush. I've passed the point of nighttime bike rides, but hope to take my son on a moonlight hike. There are few adventures as ethereal to remind one of the greatness of the universe.

5. Fix a fun drink: Folks use summertime as an excuse to make all sorts of interesting drinks. Sun tea, crazy concoctions of Kool-Aid, iced tea with a kick, Coke floats and more. I've been re-reading "Smokehouse Ham, Spoon Bread, & Scuppernong Wine: The Folklore and Art of Southern Appalachian Cooking" by my friend Joe Dabney and discovered some great old-timey recipes in there. I think I will pass on the Sumac wine and the Peach Beer, but might give some of the elderberry wines or brandies a shot. (As an aside, if you haven't read Joe's masterpiece, I strongly encourage it. It is a prime place to find great recipes and engaging stories.)

So what's on your summer bucket list? You'd better make one soon. It'll be over before you know it.

It's the end of **REM** as we know it
...and I don't feel so fine

The news of Athens-born REM breaking up is now over a week old, but many are still in a dismal mood over the news.

I am one of them.

As I've heard many folks lament, the band was the soundtrack to part of their lives. Especially for many Gen-Xers like myself, it was music that transcended the formative time from junior high to the post-college years. I think many fans can describe what was happening in their life when a certain REM album was released, who they were in love with when a particular song climbed the charts or what they were doing when they first saw a new video by the group.

I first heard REM in 1986, when, for no better reason than reading they were a great band in a music magazine, I bought their seminal work, "Life's Rich Pageant." At 13, their music along with fellow college rock groups – before they were dubbed "alternative" – U2, Simple Minds and others provided a welcome retreat from the world of adolescence and the plastic, gimmicky 80s world of hair metal and sugary pop music.

Playing in a band throughout high school and college, we always had several REM songs in our back pocket. They were easy to learn, fun to perform and the crowd always loved them.

I saw REM play three times – twice in Columbia, S.C. and once in Macon where they filmed portions of their "tourFilm" movie.

I also visited the small Georgia hamlet of Philomath once just because the band sang about it in, "Can't Get There From Here." My father indulged me and we drove through the town on the way back from a UGA football game where we watched an abandoned house burn on the side of the highway. A strange, yet poignant, memory all because of a song by REM.

I fell in and out of love with the band throughout the past 25 years. I love their early stuff, hated the "Green" album, ignored them for about five years and then, after borrowing my brother's copy of "Automatic for the People," developed a new respect for the quartet and have been a dedicated follower ever since.

This is my story on REM.

But there is a more significant story here, too.

REM helped put Southern rock music back on the map in the 1980s.

The South has a great lineage of music. We gave the world blues, rock n' roll and jazz. Yes, others may have taken it and refined it, but the roots are here. For most of the 20th century, rock music from the South was ever-present on the pop charts. But something seems to have been lost in the '70s and early '80s. The Allman Brothers had faded quite a bit after their multiple tragedies, as had fellow Southern rockers Lynyrd Skynryd.

Other rock bands from the South, with the exception of a rare single here and there by bands such as the Georgia Satellites, were playing forgettable music to an un-listening nation. And one can barely blame the critics or the public. Outside of the surge in Country Music, there just wasn't a ton of rock n' roll coming out of the South at the time.

But REM blew open the doors on that. Starting with critical acclaim for 1983's "Murmur" to their ascendancy with chart-topping songs, "The One I Love," "Stand" and "Losing My Religion," everyone knew about Athens, Ga. for reasons outside of Herschel Walker. Granted, while some groups like the B-52s were already gaining a following, it was REM's over-the-top burst that helped boost and re-boost acts that were already in Athens to more of a national prominence.

But their success didn't only help bands from Athens. In just a 10-year period from 1989, when "Green" was released, to 1999, a creative musical Renaissance occurred down here and dozens of Southern rock bands achieved national success.

The list from that period is too long to name but here are just a few you might recognize: Widespread Panic, Hootie and The Blowfish, The Black Crowes, Dillon Fence, Edwin McCain, Drivin n' Cryin', Matthew Sweet, Squirrel Nut Zippers and Ben Folds Five.

None of these bands sound the same. This isn't a list of REM knock-offs. And this list doesn't even begin to touch the music from the South that has occurred since 1999, including Neo Bluegrass to the extremely successful hip-hop genre.

But I think it does say something about what REM's success did for the South. It let the world know we all weren't only listening to and playing Country and Western or living in a "Deliverance" world, but had some creative, innovative music that no one else did.

And, not only was it original, it was good, catchy and, yes, you could dance to it.

I know it was never REM's intention to promote Southern music when they formed a band.

But, it was a great side effect.

God knows we need all the help we can get down here to remind folks we are just as artistic as the rest of the nation.

So, thanks Michael, Peter, Bill and Mike for more reasons than one.

It's been a great ride.

Mexican Fruitcake and Aunt Shirley's Orange Balls

In late May, I was laid up with a broken toe for about a month.

After unsuccessfully and stubbornly trying to continue to garden and work in the yard – two of my favorite summer activities – I decided the broken toe was a message from the Big Man to take it easy.

So I decided to dig out my acrylic paints and created some very odd abstract paintings any psychiatrist would have a field day with.

I also decided to work some more on my fiction writing.

But, most of all, I devoted my time to another favorite summer past time most of us enjoy – reading.

One evening, after a week or so, I was getting bogged down and tired of the heavy books I had been reading. I had plowed through a couple of depressing novels, reread bits and pieces of John Keats and even delved back into the weirdly titled, "The History of The Irish Race." Searching for something lighter to read, I dug into our rack of magazines. I read my weekly New Yorker (yes, I admittedly like to keep up-to-date on Eastern Elitism), a Southern Living and even my wife's Redbook in which I discovered that women, bless their hearts, still don't have the darndest idea on what to get a man for Father's Day.

At the bottom of the bin, though, was a treasure - a cookbook from my grandmother's church, First Baptist Church of Thomaston, Ga.

If you've ever owned one of these church-produced cookbooks, you know what a treasure they are. They contain recipes from just about everybody in the congregation, are filled with traditional dishes you have a hard time finding at most restaurants and have the greatest names ever assigned to dishes.

If you haven't owned one and get the bulk of your recipes off the Internet or from Martha Stewart, let me show how you're missing out.

First of all, there are the names of the dishes.

Here are a few of my favorites I found:

Mexican Fruitcake.
Aunt Shirley's Orange Balls.
Depression Cracker Pie.

Can you really beat that for names of dishes? I doubt the creative and marketing geniuses at half the chain restaurants today could develop dishes as unique sounding.

Then there are the dishes that have peoples' names attached to them. However, when you look closely at who actually submitted the recipe it is from a different person. Here is an example: "Mary Norris' Meat Loaf" recipe is submitted by Sue Lewis. Think about it. Call me sentimental, but you know there is a story there. Was Mary Norris an old friend or neighbor of Sue Lewis? How did Sue Lewis get that recipe? Is it a tribute to an old friend? There are others as well like "Bumgarner's Okra Casserole" submitted by Betty Ann Fordham and "Hazel's Jalapeno Cornbread" submitted by Brenda Barnes.

Of course, the dishes themselves are center stage here. God

bless the South, but virtually none of them are health-conscious. That said, they all sound dang good.

Beef Stew Meat with Red Gravy.
Vidalia Onion Casserole.
Million Dollar Fudge Pie.

The list goes on and on.

Being a fairly pedestrian cook, I haven't tackled any of the hundred or so recipes in the cookbook. However, I have bookmarked a couple and made not-so-subtle recommendations to my wife that they could make a fine Sunday afternoon meal.

In the meantime, I might just have to coax my grandmother to make the best recipe of all in the book, "Louise Maguire's Chocolate Fudge Cake."

And, grandmother, when you read this, just let me know when you feel inspired to bake and I will mark a day on my calendar and drive over, my wife and two sons in tow. I also promise to keep up the tradition of my father and my late granddaddy to do everything I can do in the kitchen to stay out of the way, make observations about the local newspaper and sneak tastes of the icing when you aren't looking.

The Name is Bond...
slightly-censored, fast-forwarded
...James Bond

I might be the only father in America who hasn't seen the movie "Frozen." And I can state quite honestly I haven't even heard the song "Let it Go."

I've heard the movie and song referenced, but through some strange vortex in the space-time continuum, I have been spared the songs that parents I know say make them a tad loony.

And the vortex I inhabit is because of having two sons who have little interest in princesses or ice skating, or whatever else that movie is about.

If this sounds smug, I should apologize, but I will take my small victories where I can these days.

That said, I haven't been safe from all childhood movies and their accompanying soundtracks. For much of 2013 and 2014, I heard the "Lego" theme song, "Everything is Awesome" over and over. And over and over. Again and again.

However, in the past several months, my oldest son Patrick, turning 9 this month, is entering a new phase of movies focused strictly on action and adventure. (My youngest – at 7 - still doesn't have the attention span for a complete movie).

Granted, Patrick and I have always enjoyed the "Star Wars" movies and their endless spin-offs. I even tried to tempt him to "Star Trek," perhaps to whet his science appetite. But, like his dad, he prefers Darth Vader to dark matter and Kenobi to Kirk. He also said he couldn't take a spaceship that looks like a dinner plate with two cell phones attached seriously. I tend to agree. No offense to The Enterprise, trekkies. His words, not mine.

So, with the science fiction genre on his radar, he was ready to explore more films with action and less with cartoons.

We enjoyed the usual sword and bows and arrows films such as "Troy" and "King Arthur" – pieces not too gory, and with somewhat of a story and the occasional moral compass. But, then Mr. Bond, James, that is, walked into the picture.

Patrick had seen a few scenes from Bond movies here and there and, like most boys his age, loved the gadgets, the action, the larger-than-life villains and the overall smoothness of 007.

When he discovered in January that Netflix was withdrawing their James Bond films, we went on a binge watching fest.

I was pepped to show him my two favorite Bond movies, "Goldfinger" and "Skyfall." I also steeled myself to suffer through a fit of beyond-average-Bond hijinks during the Roger Moore period and I even gained a new respect for the dark Bond, Timothy Dalton.

It was fun introducing Patrick to the great Bond villains, pointing out to him how Bond was always polite, even when deadly, how he possessed an unparalleled wit and, of course, admiring the great gadgets he had. I also discovered, watching Bond with a 9-year-old provides a few challenges, mainly the "cuddle scenes" as I call them. You know when Bond and one of his, shall we say, "lady friends," have an embrace per se. That was when I learned to quickly fast-forward through these scenes, explaining to Patrick, "This is a really boring scene, they just cuddle and hug and talk about dresses."

Of course, I had forgotten how many "cuddle scenes" old rascally James had in each movie. Goodness. Fast-forwarding actually shortened each movie by about 20 minutes. I would almost feel guilty, but, then again, my father took me to the theater to see James Bond movies – and he was a Baptist minister.

The good news is that through the years Bond has become less promiscuous since Daniel Craig took over the role and the female characters tend to get portrayed in a stronger light, especially with the grand Dame Judi Dench as M.

That all bodes well for me, of course. The next Bond movie, "Spectre" is slated to hit the theaters later this year.

I hope to take Patrick. In the theater, though, there is no way to fast-forward any racy scenes.

I reckon I'll have to use my hands. As they said in "Skyfall," "Sometimes the old ways are the best ways."

Fore whom the green never calls

Golf. Oh, golf. I really should be a good golfer. At worst, a decent duffer, but somehow I missed out on that skill.

My Uncle Bruce is an excellent golfer — so much that he not only earned a scholarship to Austin Peay University for his talent, but won several mid-major tournaments in the early 1980s.

My great-grandfather was a heck of a golfer, too, who always bragged he could shoot his age — one of the last times he did so was on his 90th birthday, when, yes, he shot under 90.

My granddaddy, Harold Maguire, frequently hit the greens and I caddied for him a few times. He passed away in 1990. My other grandfather — PopPop Wallace — still golfs. He will be 90 this fall.

And my brother is a good golfer.

I had my first experience as a golfer roughly 30 years ago. I was with my granddaddy Harold and we golfed at Thomaston Country Club in Upson County along with my brother, Jonathan. I remember it was in late June. I remember it was early in the day so that the dew on the fairway coupled with the humidity in the air made it uncomfortable at best. I remember we walked the course — an unspoken family rule was Maguires never rode in carts.

I also remember I shot a 91. The only problem was that score of 91 was only on nine holes. For those of you not familiar with golf, that score on nine holes could be kindly dubbed as 'abysmal.'

I tried a couple of more times through the years to catch the golf bug — the last time roughly a decade ago — but still could not quite "get it." I understand the concept of physics of the swing, the concentration, the focus and the "touch." And I respect those who can really golf well. But, me, well…I just missed inheriting that gene.

A few years ago, I had my own idea for an adaptation of golf. Instead of clubs, you could use crossbows, attach the golf ball onto the end of an arrow, light the balls on fire and then shoot them at the hole. Instead of walking the course or using carts, you would gallop on a horse or pedal a mountain bike. I share this idea with friends about once a year when the subject of golf comes up. For those who know me, I get the usual looks of "That's Maguire being Maguire," and the conversation moves on. For those who don't know me, well, let's just say I haven't gotten any takers yet.

But there is hope for me on the greens, yet. I have recently heard of footgolf, a new sport where golf is played, but with substituting a soccer ball.

The holes are larger and no clubs are used. I am not a very good soccer player, but I can quite happily kick the stuffing out of a ball.

I am sure I would find it a great stress relief and, worse-case scenario, I would relish being outside in nature on a piece of finely manicured land.

Until I get that invite, I will, as a public service, continue to stay away from golf courses and the closest I will get to golf is catching a cat nap while a match is on the TV during a Sunday afternoon. In advance, you're welcome.

Wolf Peach and Early Girl

Big Boy. Early Girl. Velvet Red.
Snowberry. Red Star.

These are just a few of the distinctive names culled from the tomato family and each summer I am usually blessed enough to have a few of these tasty and wonderfully-named fruits grace my garden.

I have always harbored a special fondness for tomatoes and, especially, tomato plants. I imagine it began with the unique scent the plants possess and I have traced my affinity for it back roughly 40 years ago when I would spend a couple of weeks each summer at my Maguire grandparents' home in Thomaston, Georgia. There, each summer, my granddaddy (a gentleman farmer before the term became trendy) would labor like the devil to get any growth from that stubborn clay soil. As my grandmother reminisced on red clay, "We would dig a hole, fill it up with water, and then come back three days later and the water was still there."

Regardless of the stubborn soil or the heat, my granddaddy

always coaxed several tomato plants from his garden. Spending time outdoors with him in and around his vegetable garden planted in my fertile mind a love for the sensory delights of tomatoes and their vines.

Through the years, my affinity for the homegrown red delights has only increased.

Around ten years ago, my wife and I moved next door to the late and great Henry and Iris Atkins of Smyrna. The Atkins not only taught me much about life and faith, but also awakened a dormant gardener in me by re-introducing me to the sublimity of a home-grown tomato.

I soon began growing my own and was addicted. If nothing else, I found a sublime peace in nostalgia by rubbing my fingers along the stems of the plants and then inhaling deeply, transporting my soul back to being a toddler at my granddaddy's feet as he picked and plucked and hoed his tomatoes.

During the last few years, my interest in the fruit (a term I still can't honestly say without thinking how is it not a vegetable?) has expounded into the wonderful world of tomato varieties and, subsequently, their names. The Big Boys. The Early Girls. The Velvet Reds and literally the thousands of other names I don't have the space to mention.

I did a small amount of research for this column on the etymology of tomatoes and dug up some interesting facts.

>>>The tomato's Latin name is lycopersicum which means "wolf peach." Yes, wolf peach - and is derived from German werewolf myths. These legends said a deadly nightshade plant was used by witches and sorcerers in potions to transform themselves into were-wolves, so the tomato's similar, but much larger, fruit was called the "wolf peach" when it arrived in Europe from South America. How's that for interesting? I am glad we stuck with the native moni-ker 'Tomato' instead of 'Wolf Peach.'

>>>The aforementioned native moniker is 'Tomatillo' and hails from South America. The tomato was introduced to Western civili-zation from that part of the world where we translated the name to

its current form.

>>>All in all, there are over 7,500 tomato varieties that range from your basic beefsteak to your yellow maters, Romas and the endless variety of heirlooms and hybrids.

These days, we take the tomato for granted. It's in everything: Pizza, ketchup, Italian food, sauces, Bloody Mary's and hundreds of more foods. Our society also developed the hothouse tomato phenomena, which, though the taste is a pale comparison to the real deal, still finds its way to tables across America on a daily basis.

For me, I don't eat a lot of ketchup and order my food in restaurants without tomatoes. I will only eat them in the summer and only if they are truly homegrown.

They not only taste better straight from the garden, but they're juicier and have more character in their shapes and sizes.

But, I suspect another part of it is that it takes me back to spending summers at my grandparents' home, piddling in the garden, the thick scent of tomato plants hanging in the humid air and a sense of wonder with the world. Somewhere as I dabble in my own plot, I imagine I try to catch a bit of that feeling.

A lost stab at innocence and maybe even imagine the spirit of my granddaddy smiling on me.

About the Author

Raised as a preacher's son, Mark Wallace Maguire grew up throughout the Southeast living in cities and towns across Georgia, North Carolina, Alabama, Kentucky and South Carolina. He's worked in newspapers and magazines for over 18 years and been honored with over a dozen awards for his work from many organizations including the Society for Professional Journalists, Georgia Poetry Society and Georgia Associated Press. In 2005, he was named Young Outstanding Alumni of the Year for Berry College. He lives south of Atlanta in Red Clay Country with his wife and two sons. You can read more about him at www.markwallacemaguire.com

Made in the USA
Lexington, KY
25 October 2015